The Library of
E-Commerce and Internet Careers

Careers with Successful Dot-Com Companies

Tonya Buell

The Rosen Publishing Group, Inc.
New York

Published in 2001 by The Rosen Publishing Group, Inc.
29 East 21st Street, New York, NY 10010

Library of Congress Cataloging-in-Publication Data

Buell, Tonya.
Careers with successful dot-com companies/by Tonya Buell. — 1st ed.
p. cm. — (The library of e-commerce and Internet careers)
Includes bibliographical references and index.
ISBN 0-8239-3424-1 (library binding)
1. Electronic commerce—Vocational guidance—Juvenile literature. 2. Internet industry—Vocational guidance—Juvenile literature. [1. Electronic commerce. 2. Internet industry—Vocational guidance. 3. Vocational guidance.] I. Title. II. Series.
HF5548.32 .B82 2001
004.67'8'02373—dc21

00-012748

Manufactured in the United States of America

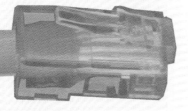

Table of Contents

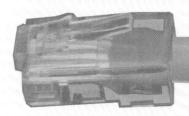

Introduction

The Internet is revolutionizing the world. Imagine writing all of your letters on paper instead of using e-mail, spending your Saturdays in a dusty library researching term papers, and having to go to the mall to buy your favorite CDs. That was the world before the Internet.

Just over five years ago, the Internet was a brand-new concept. Universities and the government had used it for many years, but software and services weren't available for the general public to use. Now the Internet is everywhere, and it is not going away. In fact, it's getting much bigger.

In addition to changing the way we do things, the Internet has also created a large number of career and business opportunities. The exchange of money over the Internet is called electronic commerce, or "e-commerce." In addition to "pure-plays" (businesses that operate only online) such as

Amazon.com, many retailers that have operated offline in physical stores for years have now added an online component to their businesses. New e-commerce companies need employees with skills specially suited to electronic businesses. And there are many opportunities for new small businesses.

In 1995, Pierre Omidyar had a problem. His girlfriend collected Pez dispensers, but had no place to buy and sell them easily. He decided to create a Web site where people could sell things, all kinds of things, and other people could log on and buy them. He named the Web site eBay, originally thinking of it as a tool his neighborhood could use. Today, eBay is one of the largest and most successful e-commerce sites on the Internet. Pierre Omidyar is a billionaire.

Like Pierre Omidyar, you may have a new idea for a Web site. Your business may start out small, but could grow into a very successful corporation. One of the advantages an Internet company has is the ability to reach an almost unlimited number of people. If a shoe store opens in your neighborhood, only people who live near the store will be able to visit it and purchase shoes. However, if a store opens up shop online, it can reach anyone in the world who uses the

One of the most successful e-commerce startups is eBay.com. Here, eBay chief executive Meg Whitman chats with Pierre Omidyar, eBay's chairman and founder.

Internet—and that number is rapidly growing. It is possible to grow a small business into a multinational corporation, especially when all of the business is conducted over the Internet.

NOT WITHOUT RISK

Because of its unparalleled success during the past few years, employees raced to join the e-commerce industry. New Internet businesses started up every day. Now, as dot-coms seem to be folding left and right, everyone not involved in their success is more than happy to comment on their downfall.

The truth is, it's still too early to judge whether all these defeated dot-coms were a result of too many Internet businesses, or simply poorly run companies founded on shaky ideas. Just as with traditional businesses, for every triumph such as Amazon.com, there are more than a few failures, such as Eve.com, Boo.com, and Garden.com.

Whether or not a dot-com company is a success, there is still much to learn from working for one. Even those e-commerce employees who have found themselves out of a job agree that they would not trade the experience they gained for anything. Many have been heavily recruited by companies still in business. However, this means that seasoned workers are now competing for fewer jobs. Therefore, it is best to be prepared—to possess marketable skills and experience, and to make smart choices. All of this will prepare you for the next wave of successful dot-com companies.

The e-commerce world is growing and changing at breakneck speed. By the time you're ready to look for a job, the market might have risen and fallen two or three more times. That's why the industry is so risky, and why it's also so exciting.

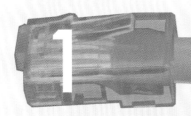

Dot-Com
Startup Companies

A dot-com company is a company that does most or all of its business over the Internet. E-commerce companies are dot-com companies that allow people to buy, sell, or barter goods and services over the Internet.

A dot-com startup is a new dot-com company. How new is new, you ask? Well, they say that one year in the Internet world equals seven years in the regular world. So a dot-com company that's been around for two years is fourteen years old by traditional standards—not exactly a new company. Since most traditional companies that are a few years old are still considered new, a dot-com company that has opened its cyberdoors within the past six months is new, and is definitely a dot-com startup.

Like traditional businesses, new dot-com companies must do a lot of planning and preparation before opening their "doors" to the general public. A dot-com startup may not even have a Web site at first, just a good idea or a couple of people with a business plan. If you join a dot-com startup at a very early stage, you will get to help build the business from nothing. This is an exciting but challenging proposition, since you'll get to make important decisions and create something out of nothing.

NOT YOUR TRADITIONAL BUSINESS

Dot-com startups are very different from other types of companies. Because the online world is growing very rapidly, things within dot-com start-ups change all the time. There is always plenty of work to do and plenty to learn. If the startup is understaffed or unprepared for certain needs that pop up, employees will have to do several different jobs at once.

Traditional businesses and established dot-com companies are usually very organized and steady in their work. Dot-com startups, however, are just learning how to do everything for the first time. Often, no other company has done what they're doing, which means that there are no rules. Everything is brand new. At a dot-com startup, you may work on a completely new idea, or learn to use a brand-new technology, but you definitely won't be bored.

WHAT TO EXPECT IN THE FUTURE

As the world of e-commerce grows, new dot-com businesses will be able to use established dot-coms as models. By examining how other startups have or have not worked, a new dot-com business may avoid falling into traps that lead to failure. For example, Pets.com was started in 1998 to sell pet supplies online and instantly became well-known for the popular "Sock Puppet" television advertisements. However popular Pets.com became, it simply did not make enough money to pay for all of its expenses. Eventually, in November 2000, Pets.com was forced to close its cyberdoors.

PetSmart.com, which was started mid-1999, also used the idea of selling pet supplies online, but decided to work with an existing pet store (PetSmart) to help it make sales at a lower cost.

PetSmart.com sells pet supplies online in conjunction with existing stores. Usually, having a physical store can boost sales for a dot-com business.

The e-commerce world is seeing that bolstering an e-tailer with a physical store can solidify a business and increase sales.

At the same time, new e-businesses will be able to start and grow with less effort. Technology will become more powerful and simpler to learn and use, and tools will be created to do everything from promoting a Web business to building a powerful e-commerce site without having to do any programming.

E-Commerce Successes and Failures

The e-commerce world is filled with ups and downs. Some companies experience wild success, while others crash and burn.

The successful . . .

➤ Amazon.com started out selling books and has expanded to selling just about everything.

➤ eBay was started by one man, working from his home, and is now a multibillion dollar auction extravaganza.

➤ Overstock.com, a company that sells closeout items at cut-rate prices, is one of the first large Internet retailers to make a profit!

And the not-so-successful . . .

➤ Pets.com had a popular sock puppet, but not enough sales.

➤ PlanetRx, a site based on health care, died a slow death before partnering with drugstore.com.

➤ Garden.com, which was created to sell garden supplies online, closed its cyberdoors in November 2000.

➤ Eve.com began selling cosmetics online in the middle of 1999 and stopped a year later.

Eventually, starting a new e-commerce company will be similar to starting a traditional business. Some businesses will succeed, and some will fail, but they will all try to attract customers, provide the best products, and make a good profit.

WORKING AT DOT-COM STARTUPS

John is very independent and wants to work at a dot-com startup. He doesn't think he'd like programming computers, though, and he's not really a "techie." John likes to work with people.

Mary loves everything about e-commerce and the Internet. She got her first computer when she was ten and built her first Web site when she was twelve. Mary loves figuring out how the computer works and learning new things. She can sit at the computer for hours.

Tim likes computers, but he likes art, too. He doesn't know if he wants to do technical or programming work—he'd prefer to do something more creative. Tim is very artistic and would like to use this talent in his career.

There are three basic types of careers within dot-com startup companies: business and management careers, engineering and technical careers, and design and artistic careers. You don't have to be a techie to work at a dot-com startup. John might pursue a business or management career, Mary a technical career, and Tim an artistic career.

At smaller startup companies, one person may play all three roles. Or, if two people start a business together, one person may do the business part, one the technical part, and they may hire a freelance artist for the artistic part. Large startup companies will hire many people in each of the three areas.

Working at a dot-com startup is a little like riding on a roller coaster in the dark: it's a fun and exciting ride, it's a little scary, and you never know what's around the corner. The good news is that you'll get to learn lots of new things, make your own rules, and benefit when the company succeeds. The bad news is that you will often work long hours and feel like your work is never done. You also may find one day that your company has gone out of business without warning.

Business and Management Careers

B usiness and management careers within new e-commerce companies require people who can think and make decisions quickly, who are very people-oriented, and who can come up with new ideas and concepts on their own. These careers range from a Web entrepreneur, who comes up with the idea and starts the business, to a customer service representative, who answers customers' questions, to a product manager, who decides what products to sell and how to market them.

EDUCATION AND TRAINING

Business and management careers require a combination of technical and management expertise. Unlike business careers in traditional companies, which only require a business degree or work experience, these careers require Web or technical knowledge as well. A bachelor's or master's degree in business administration and a minor in computer science or some technical coursework is ideal. However, general business and technical knowledge, which can be gained through job experience and reading books, is usually enough (especially for smaller startups).

In addition, it is very important that you really know the business that you're working in. For example, if you're going to be working for a new company that is selling T-shirts over the Internet, it is very important that you know enough about T-shirts to make important decisions such as how much they should cost, which T-shirts to feature on the site, and which group of people you should try to sell to.

Sarah is the marketing director of a dot-com startup. She arrives at the office bright and early in order to get a head start on the day. The president of the company has asked her to try to get other similar companies to partner with them, so that they can trade links and share mailing lists. She has sent e-mails offering to discuss a partnership agreement to many different companies, and a few have responded with interest. Today, she must

Feel the Need for Speed

Joining a dot-com startup is like jumping onto a speeding train. Dot-com startups move at breakneck speeds, and you'll need to be able to keep up. When you interview with a startup, it is important that you let the interviewer know that you understand the enormous need for speed. Here are some tips to help you speed up the pace of your work.

➤ Just Do It. If you have an idea or need to do something, just do it. Now. One of the biggest time wasters is procrastination.

➤ Keep It Simple. If you're trying to start a company selling used CDs over the Internet, set up your site to sell only used CDs. Don't think about selling used DVDs, tapes, or records, or try to figure out how to add extra features to your site. Keep it simple and focus on what you're trying to accomplish.

➤ Get Organized. You need to be very organized when you're working on five tasks at once. Make a list of things you need to do and stick with it.

➤ Be Prepared. Be prepared for whatever may come your way. If you have spare time, brush up on your HTML skills or get organized. At a dot-com startup, you never know what may come up next.

respond to the e-mails with more information about the company and the type of partnership it is interested in creating. As she goes through her inbox of e-mails, she comes to one company that would also like to trade content and functionality between Web sites. She thinks this is a good idea, but is not sure if it is possible. She asks the president of her company about it, who also thinks it's a good idea. Together, they form a proposal to send to the other company. When she returns to her desk, she has several telephone messages from magazines and newspapers where her company has been advertising. She'll finish responding to her e-mails, and then get to her phone calls. Hopefully, she'll also have time for lunch!

TYPES OF BUSINESS AND MANAGEMENT CAREERS

Web Entrepreneur

A Web entrepreneur is a person who comes up with a good idea for a new e-commerce company and then starts the business. Entrepreneurs are usually very good at thinking up new and clever ideas, and they

From his home, Web entrepreneur Harry Knowles runs Ain't It Cool News, a Web site with insider news about Hollywood's latest projects.

also must have the determination to follow through with their ideas. Sometimes, a Web entrepreneur may be able to get investors or an incubator (a company that helps startups get off the ground) to help with his or her startup, and other times he or she will start it alone or with a few friends. Web entrepreneurs always start with nothing but an idea and then put a plan into action to make it a reality. They must also have the ability to work and make decisions extremely quickly in the fast-paced world of e-commerce.

Project Manager

A project manager oversees the creation of the e-commerce Web site. He or she needs to coordinate work between the entrepreneur and the technical and artistic people to ensure that a quality site is built within the time and budget allowed. This means that he or she should know a little about almost everything, including technical, financial, artistic, and business issues. Since the project manager is ultimately responsible for the Web site, he or she must have strong leadership skills and must be very efficient and dependable.

Product Manager

A product manager determines what products to sell, to whom, and for how much. He or she should know a lot about the type of products the company is selling, the customers, and the competition. Will customers prefer to buy one product instead of another similar product? Do the products being sold make sense together? For example, a product manager would probably not want to try to sell winter coats and bathing suits on the same Web page, unless there was a very good reason.

Marketing Director

A marketing director decides how to bring people to the Web site and how to get the people to buy once they're at the site. He or she determines what type of marketing is best for the business. The marketing director of a company selling baby food, for example, must decide if it's smarter to buy a Super Bowl television advertisement or to advertise in a parenting magazine. A marketing director with a limited budget must think creatively to reach as many potential customers as possible.

Customer Service Representative

A customer service representative answers questions and guides customers through a company's Web site. Customer service representatives may help customers over the telephone, through e-mail, or directly on the Web site by acting as a "virtual customer assistant." People in this job should be very friendly and service-oriented. Customer service representatives should also know a lot about the products the company sells and about the company's Web site.

Engineering and Technical Careers

E ngineering and technical careers within a dot-com company require technical people who can turn a good idea into a technical solution. In these jobs, you may need to build a complete Web site from scratch, which means you should have strong design and planning skills as well as technical skills. Since, especially at smaller startups, one person may play two or three (or all) of the technical roles, it is important that technical people be able to learn new things very quickly.

Engineering and technical careers also often require lots of time. Although just about everybody at a dot-com startup will work very hard and will be expected to put in far more than the average forty hours per week, this is especially true of the technical people. Dot-com companies usually try to build a Web site or piece of software that should take months or years in a fraction of that time. It is important, therefore, that you are able to work quickly and steadily, and it is especially important that you really love your work.

EDUCATION AND TRAINING

Engineering and technical careers require lots and lots of technical knowledge. They also require you to have specific knowledge about the current technologies, which means that you must be able to learn quickly and teach yourself new things.

Most dot-com companies would rather hire technical people who have a computer science degree than people with any other type of degree. If you're planning on working at a larger dot-com startup, a computer science degree and experience in the latest technologies is perfect. If you want to be a lead technical person, you might need business and management education as well. Many chief technology officers have a bachelor's degree in computer science and a master's degree in business administration (an MBA).

It is also very important that you have development experience that you can describe or show to the company, even if it is just a project you completed in school or a Web site you built with your friends.

Engineering and technical careers require a lot of specific training. Most dot-com companies prefer employees who have a college degree in computer science.

Companies want to see if you can actually do what you went to school for, and this is especially true for dot-com startups, since you won't get the on-the-job training that established companies offer.

Jay is a software developer at a fledgling dot-com company. He arrives at work in the late morning, since he usually stays well into the evening. Last night the technical team had a meeting to discuss problems with how the Web site was working, and they made a list of each problem and who would fix it.

After pouring himself a large cup of coffee, Jay tackles the first problem on his list: The Web site isn't saving enough information about the user when the user signs up for the company's mailing list. Jay looks through the programs to pinpoint exactly where the problem is occurring. He studies the program to determine the best way to fix the problem. Then he notices that this fix will require a change in the database, so he asks the database administrator to make that change. Finally, he makes the fix in the program and tests it. It seems to work! Now, Jay hands the program over to the QA (quality assurance) manager for further testing and marks that

How Techies Spend Their Days... and Sometimes Nights

Ever wonder what techies do all day? Have you seen them, pounding away at the computer for hours, but don't know what they're really doing?

Computers are very picky and not very smart. If you've ever encountered a weird error message on a Web page, or had to restart your computer because it froze, you've seen examples of computer programs that didn't work.

Writing these programs is like solving many different puzzles. Now imagine that each of those puzzles is also part of one larger puzzle. That's what building an entire e-commerce site is like. There are many different ways to solve each problem, and the goal is to find the best way. But it is also necessary to think about how each problem fits into the larger puzzle, because if that isn't solved, then nothing is.

Techies spend their days coming up with solutions to each of the little puzzles and testing to make sure that their solutions help solve the big puzzle, too. Technical people must be very creative to come up with solutions to all of the different puzzles that they're given.

*task off his list. He'll work on the next few
tasks and then start a game of Ping-Pong
with a few of his coworkers.*

TYPES OF ENGINEERING AND TECHNICAL CAREERS

Web Developer

A Web developer creates the part of the Web site
that you can see. He or she writes instructions that
tell the computer to make a link to send a person to
another part of the Web site, to make a picture and
words appear on the same page, and to make everything on the site line up properly and look right.
This means that a Web developer must have design
and creativity skills as well as technical skills. After
the designer (described in chapter 4) decides how
things will look on the Web site, the Web developer
makes it happen.

Software Developer

A software developer programs the part of the Web
site that does things. He or she might create a shopping cart program to calculate how much money the
customer owes, or design and build a system to
remember everything a person has ever ordered.

The important difference between a software developer and a Web developer is that a software developer programs things that happen behind the scenes on the Web site, while a Web developer programs the things that everyone can see. A software developer should have very strong programming and technical skills, and should know the latest programming languages.

QA Manager/Tester

A QA manager tests the Web site to make sure that everything works properly. QA stands for quality assurance, meaning that this person makes sure the Web site is a high-quality site. If you've ever surfed the Web and found links that lead to nowhere, strange error messages, or programs that just plain don't work, you've probably found a company that needs better quality assurance. A QA manager needs to establish a very careful plan to make sure that every part of the site is tested and that things are retested when changes are made. This person should be very detail-oriented.

Database Administrator

A database administrator (sometimes called a DBA) creates and looks after the Web site's database. A database is the place where the information for the site is stored. For example, a Web site selling shoes over the Internet will have a large catalog of all of the shoes that it sells stored in the database. This database would contain information such as the name of each shoe, a picture, the sizes available, and the price of the shoe.

System Administrator

A system administrator looks after the operating system where the Web site exists. An operating system is the software that makes your computer run, such as Microsoft Windows. The system administrator must make sure that the Web site is up and running all of the time, that it operates quickly, and that it is secure from computer criminals.

Design and
Artistic Careers

P eople in design and artistic careers create the look and feel of the Web site. They design logos and banners to advertise the site, and decide where things like pictures, arrows, buttons, or bullets should be placed. They need to design a very attractive site that makes people want to buy, but they also need to consider things such as how fast the site loads onto someone's computer. For example, a lot of pictures may look nice but might also make the site load very slowly. Therefore, design and artistic people should have some technical knowledge in addition to artistic skills.

Artistic people at dot-com startups also need to know a lot about the company's products and customers. They need to be able to design a site that fits both. An e-commerce company selling rugged adventure gear, for example, would probably not have pastel-colored flowers and cursive writing, while a site selling wedding accessories would probably not be dark with bold lettering.

EDUCATION AND TRAINING

Design and artistic careers require artistic knowledge as well as technical skills. A bachelor's or master's degree in design is very useful for these careers, though not mandatory. Web design and graphics design classes are probably offered at your local community college or through a learning center. These classes will teach you design and prepare you for college while familiarizing you with the latest design software.

Artistic careers at dot-com companies also require lots of experience. For practice, you should create some sample Web sites, which will also show companies your artistic and technical skills. Employers might also want to see your sample drawings, pictures, and images.

Julie is a Web designer for a dot-com start-up. The startup already has a Web site, but has asked Julie to change it to make it look

A career as a Web designer requires artistic and technical skills. Web design and graphic design classes are helpful for a career in e-commerce.

more attractive and professional. She has come up with several different ideas for the basic layout, fonts, and colors for the home page, and reviewed them with the president of the company, who liked one style in particular.

Today Julie is designing the layout of the product pages, using the same colors and style as the home page. First, she meets briefly with the marketing director and product managers to get a general idea of how they would like the products organized on the site. As she sits down to begin creating a sample layout, she realizes that it would be nice to have "Buy Now" and "Shopping Cart" buttons that match the company logo. She asks the graphic artist to design the buttons and continues creating a layout. She decides that there should not be more than five or six products per page, and wherever possible, there should be a picture of the product. She arranges the products in two columns, with the name, description, and price of each product underneath its picture. She adds the company logo and a gray bar at the top of the page with bold text containing the title of the page. The page looks nice, but she still feels it's missing something. After a short break for lunch, she'll meet with the graphic artist to come up with small icons or pictures to make the page even more attractive.

TYPES OF DESIGN AND ARTISTIC CAREERS

Graphic Artist

A graphic artist creates the company logo, draws the pictures, and designs the buttons, arrows, and

Web Design Tips and Tools

So, you want to be a Web designer? Dot-com startups are always in need of good designers who can make their site look attractive and make customers want to buy. E-commerce Web sites should be simple, easy to use, and clear. As a graphic or Web designer, it will be your job to make sure that the Web site looks nice, is easy to use, and loads and runs quickly.

Web and graphic designers must be familiar with the latest versions of graphic design and Web design software. Take a class or teach yourself how to use the following design tools and you'll be one step ahead of the game!

➤ Photoshop is a graphic design tool that allows you to draw and edit pictures, logos, and other images.

➤ Freehand is another widely used graphic design tool similar to Photoshop.

➤ Flash is a tool that allows to you create animations and moving pictures for the Web.

➤ FrontPage and Dreamweaver are Web design tools that allow you to create a Web page and preview how it will look.

lines that are to be placed on the Web site. This person must be able to create all of the images that make a Web site look attractive. He or she will work with the designer and the Web developer to decide what pictures should be on the site and how they should look.

The graphic artist should be very familiar with the latest graphic design tools such as Photoshop and Freehand, and should understand how to create graphics for the Web. For example, pictures and logos created for Web pages need to be small in size (for fast loading), should contain only Web-friendly colors, and should be in .gif or .jpg format.

Designer

A designer decides how the e-commerce Web site will appear. He or she decides what colors to use, what pictures to use, and where everything should fit on the Web page. In addition to having lots of artistic and design skills, designers must know how to make an attractive and professional-looking Web site that will make people want to buy. They should also have Web development skills and be familiar with Web development tools such as Frontpage and Dreamweaver, as they will work very closely with the Web developer to create the basic Web pages.

A Web designer should also understand how different colors and images look in different browsers. The same Web page may look completely different to someone using WebTV than it does to someone using Internet Explorer, and the same applies for Netscape, America Online, and the many other browsers that are used. A Web designer must understand these differences in order to make sure the site looks good for everyone.

Starting Your Career

You can begin preparing for your career at a dot-com startup right now. No matter what type of career you want, there are lots of things that you can do that will help you learn what you'll need to know, give you the practice you need, and help you get the job you want.

TEN THINGS YOU CAN DO RIGHT NOW TO GET PREPARED

1. Teach Yourself HTML

HTML, or hypertext markup language, is the basis of every Web site, so just about everybody at a dot-com startup should know how it works. Check out an HTML book from your local library and get started.

2. Take a Web Design or Development Class

Most community colleges or local learning centers offer Web design and development classes. If they don't, ask them to start one!

3. Build a Web Site for Yourself Just for Practice

Include pictures of your friends and family, or create links to your favorite Web sites.

4. Check Out Books on the Internet from Your Local Library

There are tons of books about the Internet out there, and lots to learn. Get the books at your local library, and read them thoroughly.

5. Get Ideas About How Sites Should (and Shouldn't) Look

There are lots of good ideas out there, and some not-so-good ideas, too. Surf the Web and notice what things you like about each site and what things you don't like.

6. Offer to Build a Friend's or Neighbor's Small Business Web Site

Do any of your neighbors or parents' friends have a small business? Offer to build their Web site and you'll get good practice and make money!

7. Create a Web Site for Your School Club or Group of Friends

It could have a calendar of activities, a list of people in the club, and group pictures.

8. Make a List of Places to Find Jobs at Dot-Com Startups

Make a list of incubators, job-search sites, and other places where new dot-com companies advertise for jobs. Keep the list updated.

9. Stay on Top of New Technologies

Job-search sites describe the skills companies are looking for. Browse through Web development books at the bookstore to find out what's new.

10.Get A Part-Time Job

Get a part-time job at an e-business or a small company. Offer to build and maintain its Web site, or to add e-commerce capability to its existing site.

EXPERIENCE, EXPERIENCE, EXPERIENCE!

These days almost every company is looking for employees who have previous experience, and dot-com startups are no different. In fact, startups often place more importance on experience because they need someone who can get things done right away and with almost no on-the-job training. So how do you get that first job to get the experience you need?

New e-businesses are looking for people who can do the job. They know that you won't have five years of experience working with a technology that's only been around for two or three years. They often place less importance on the number of years of experience you have, and more importance on what you've actually done. If you can show them the Web addresses of some sites that you've built, even if they were only for yourself or school projects, the companies will be far more impressed than if you have nothing to show.

THE POWER OF A COMPUTER SCIENCE DEGREE

Although experience is a valuable tool for getting a dot-com job, most companies also prefer someone with a college degree. And for dot-com companies, you just can't beat a computer science degree.

Since you'll very likely be doing two or three (or more) different jobs at a dot-com startup, you'll need a wide variety of skills. And all of the jobs you'll be doing have one thing in common: They all require lots of technical knowledge. People in business positions need to have in-depth knowledge of the latest Web technologies in order to make decisions about what the Web site should do and what Web software to use.

Artistic people must be familiar with the latest graphic design software and multimedia tools, many of which now include programming languages for the creation of animations and moving images. A computer science degree is almost a must for technical careers.

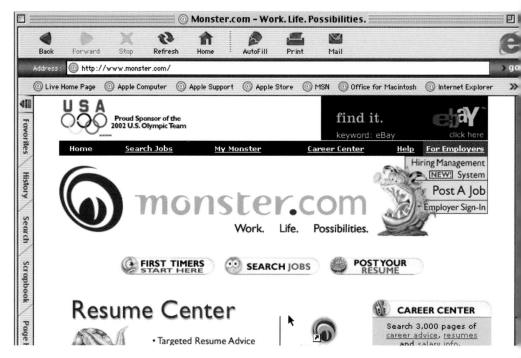

Job-search sites like Monster.com are valuable tools to help you land a job in the field of e-commerce.

PICKING A COMPANY THAT'S RIGHT FOR YOU

Startups, like people, come in all shapes and sizes. Some well-funded companies will have large departments and lots of employees, and will act more like an established company than a startup. Other companies will have just a few employees who do almost everything. Every company does things a little differently.

If you like doing lots of different things in many different areas, and you're very independent and smart, you'll probably prefer working for a smaller startup. If you like getting really good at one thing and knowing exactly what you're supposed to do, you'll prefer a larger startup.

Since you'll be working with the people at the company every day, and you often work very closely with coworkers at any small business, it is very important that you like the people at the company. When you go on a job interview, you'll probably get to meet several people. Don't just let them interview you—interview them, too, to see if you'd like working with them.

When you're ready to start looking for a job at a dot-com startup, it's time to go online and start researching companies. Job-search sites like Monster.com are an excellent place to start. Browsing through their job listings will allow you to see which companies are looking for new employees. You can also find new dot-com companies by looking at the Web sites of incubators described in chapter 6 (do a keyword search on "incubator" to find them). They often have several new Web sites starting at any given time.

NEGOTIATING SALARY AND BENEFITS PACKAGES

One major benefit of working for a dot-com startup is that they usually offer exceptional benefit packages in addition to a normal salary. These can include stock options or an employee stock purchase plan, which allows you to own a small piece of the company. Most companies should provide you with basic health insurance and paid holidays, and many will provide a retirement plan. Some companies will also offer bonuses, tuition reimbursement, a well-being program, or miscellaneous services that you should consider when determining which package is best for you.

When calculating the salary you will receive from a company, you should add up the base salary plus any money you will get from bonuses. Then you must estimate the value of stock options and an employee stock purchase plan, and add it in. Any other benefits that you will use, such as tuition reimbursement (if you plan to continue going to school in your spare time), or the retirement plan, should be added to the total package to see which company offers the best deal.

Some companies, for example, offer a lower base salary, but lots of stock options. If you think the company will become very successful, you might want to accept the lower salary because the stock options may become very valuable. However, if you have accepted a lower salary bolstered by stock options and your company's stock never gains much value, you could find yourself acquiring nothing more than experience. More often, Internet companies are offering salaries comparable to those paid by tradi-tional businesses. You may not become an instant millionaire if the company flourishes, but it will be a much less risky venture.

When comparing salary and benefits packages, you should only consider the benefits that you will actually use. Some companies try to pad their benefits packages with lots of benefits and services that are hardly ever used, just so they look better to potential employees. If you are unsure, ask a parent or trusted adult to help you determine which deal is the best for you.

Launching Your Own Startup

I f you have a good idea, and you're not afraid of hard work or the possibility of failure, why not start your own e-commerce company? It's not going to be easy, and success is not guaranteed. You can create a small Web site, or you can put together a detailed business plan and try to get people to invest in your company.

BUILDING THE BUSINESS OUT OF YOUR LIVING ROOM

You can build an entire e-commerce business out of your living room. In fact, that's one of the most exciting things about e-commerce companies. You don't need an expensive storefront or glossy brochures. Instead, you need to focus on building an attractive, professional-looking Web site, setting up order processing, spreading the word, and being able to fill orders.

There are many books and Web sites that describe how to build a Web business. (See the For More Information and For Further Reading sections at the end of this book for a partial list.) Some software and Web sites even allow you to create an entire e-commerce site without doing any programming.

If you prefer not to build the site yourself, look for a freelance Web developer to do it for you. Your parents or friends may already know a Web developer, or you may be able to find one by going to a freelance search site such as Ants.com or Guru.com. This, of course, will require money, and the

JESSICA DILULLO HERRIN AND JENNY LEFCOURT, FOUNDERS OF DELLA.COM

Jessica DiLullo Herrin and Jenny Lefcourt met at college. Jenny told Jessica that she was frustrated with buying wedding gifts for friends and family, and Jessica replied that she had always wanted to start a business selling wedding products over the Internet. The two women worked on the business plan over spring break, and launched their site, Della.com, that summer. They have now merged with WeddingChannel.com to become one of the most popular and useful wedding sites on the Internet.

amount depends on the type of site you need. You may be able to start your business with your savings, or you may be able to convince others to invest in your company.

SPREADING THE WORD

Once you build your e-commerce Web site, you'll realize that you need to spend a lot of time letting people know about it. There are millions of Web sites out there, and you want people to find yours. So how do you spread the word without spending lots of money on advertising? Here is a list of ways you can spread the word about your e-business.

1. Tell Friends and Family Members

This is the first and best place to start. Tell everyone you know, they'll tell people they know, and your site's traffic will grow.

2. Put Up Signs

You can create signs on your computer at home or at school, and then post them at local businesses around town.

3. Pass Out Flyers

Flyers are a great way to get the word out for any new business. Pass them around to neighbors and businesses.

4. Join a Banner Exchange Program

Banner exchange programs such as Microsoft's bCentral.com let you trade banner advertising with other Web sites.

5. Submit Your Site to Search Engines

Search engines are where most people find out about new Web sites. Most search engines have a small link at the bottom of their page called "Submit Your Site" where you can add your site.

6. Try to Get Gift Links

Ask other Web sites who have a similar theme to add a link to your site. If you're not competing with them and they like your site, they often will.

7. Exchange Links

Offer to add a link to another site in exchange for a link to your site. Many companies will agree to this type of exchange.

To Do List

➤ Decide on the type of
  e-business you want to launch.
➤ Plan what products to sell
  and for how much.
➤ Choose the name of the Web site
  and register it with a company such as
  Network Solutions.
➤ Decide how the Web site should look
  (colors, fonts, layout, pictures).
➤ Decide how to process orders (credit
  card, check, etc.).
➤ Build the Web site.
➤ Test the Web site completely to make
  sure there are no errors.
➤ Put the Web site online.
➤ Get a business license and a
  bank account.
➤ Tell everyone you know about the
  Web site.
➤ Submit your site to all of the major
  search engines.
➤ Pass out flyers and put up signs.
➤ Exchange banners and links with
  other sites.

WORKING WITH INVESTORS

Some small businesses try to get others to invest money in their company. An investor is a person who offers to buy a small part of the business for a certain amount of money. The person believes that the business will succeed and that he or she will get his or her money back in profits.

The All-Important Business Plan

If you would like to get someone to invest money in your company, you must have a business plan. A business plan tells the investor how you plan to make money with your business. It explains what you sell, who your customers are, and why you are better than other companies. It also contains charts and spreadsheets explaining exactly how much money you plan to make and how soon.

For example, suppose you want to sell home-made cookies over the Internet. You will sell them for $10 per bag, and you think you'll be able to sell 100 bags per month. However, you first need to pay someone $2,000 to build your Web site. You might ask an investor for $2,000 in exchange for 20 per-cent of your business. You would need to create a detailed business plan explaining what you sell, why your cookies will sell better than other cookies,

There are many Web sites that can help you create a plan to attract investors and start your business.

and how much money the investor will get back in return for his or her investment.

An effective business plan is not a prediction or a wish. It is a projection. You must try to anticipate all of your needs and everything that will happen during your first few years. It will help to talk to people who have started their own businesses. It is also important that you thoroughly research the market, as well as your concept.

There are many Web sites that can help you create a business plan. One good example is on American Express's Small Business Exchange, located at http://home3.americanexpress.com/smallbusiness/ resources/starting/biz_plan.

Angel Investors and Venture Capital

An angel investor is someone who offers to invest in a company before it has even started. Many investors prefer to invest in companies that are already on their feet and making money.

However, an angel investor may invest in you and your company before you even have a Web site or any customers.

If you have already built your site and are starting to make money, you might try to get venture capital. A venture capitalist is an investor who prefers to invest in a company that has already started, but that is still fairly new.

You may be making some money, but wish to expand your business or advertise your products. The venture capitalist will offer to buy a certain percent of your business, which will give you the money you need to advertise and expand. He or she believes that you will do well and that the company will be worth more in the future.

Incubators

Many new dot-com companies choose to get started with the help of an incubator. An incubator is a company that helps e-commerce companies get started. It helps with the accounting, legal, and technical parts of the business. Like a parent who helps a small child grow and learn how to take care of himself or herself, an incubator helps a new business learn and grow in the best way possible.

GO FOR IT

Building your own dot-com company can require more work and greater risks than you've ever imagined. You may work day and night, spend more money than you originally planned, and pull from more resources than you knew you had in you. And your company may still fail. The task is large, but if you succeed, the reward is great. Even if you build a small company that gets only a few hits and fewer sales, you will have gained experience to draw upon in the future. And, if you set your sights higher, you may be able to build the next e-commerce success story.

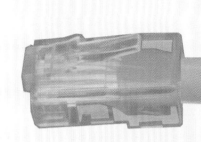

Glossary

barter   Trading one thing for another without using money.

budget   The amount of money a person or business can spend.

cyberdoor   An imaginary front door to an e-commerce business.

database   A collection of information and data in the computer.

dot-com company   A company that does most or all of its business over the Internet.

dot-com startup   A new (online six months or less) Internet company.

e-commerce   Buying, selling, or trading things over the Internet.

entrepreneur   A person who starts a new business.

HTML   Hypertext markup language, the programming code used to create a Web site.

incubator A company that helps other new e-businesses get started.

investor Someone who buys a percentage of the business, expecting the business to be successful.

program A series of instructions that tells a computer what to do.

For More Information

JOB-SEARCH SITES

CareerBuilder.com
http://www.careerbuilder.com

HotJobs.com
http://www.hotjobs.com

Monster.com
http://www.monster.com

WEB BUILDING TUTORIALS

About.com: HTML/XML
http://html.about.com/compute/html/index.htm

Build Your Own Web Site
http://build-website.com

HTML: An Interactive Tutorial for Beginners
http://www.davesite.com/webstation/html

NEW BUSINESS TOOLS

**Microsoft bCentral—online services for
small businesses**
http://www.bcentral.com

**Quicken.com—Small Business Center:
Start a Business**
http://quicken.webcrawler.com/small_business/start

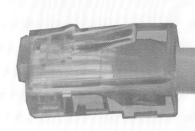

For Further Reading

Fiore, Frank. *The Complete Idiot's Guide to Starting an Online Business*. Indianapolis, IN: Que, 2000.

Kador, John. *Internet Jobs! The Complete Guide to Finding the Hottest Internet Jobs*. New York: McGraw-Hill, 2000.

Kienan, Brenda. *Small Business Solutions: E-Commerce*. Redmond, WA: Microsoft Press, 2000.

Lieber, Ron. *Upstart Start-ups!* New York: Broadway Books, 1998.

Maran, Ruth. *Creating Web Pages with HTML Simplified*. 2nd ed. Indianapolis, IN: IDG Books Worldwide, Inc., 1999.

Williams, Robin, and John Tollett. *The Non-Designer's Web Book*. 2nd ed. Berkeley, CA: Peachpit Press, 2000.

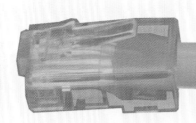

Index

ABOUT THE AUTHOR

Tonya Buell is a founder and CEO of TravelDazzle.com, an online travel and tour directory. She also worked on a number of Web development projects while employed as a software designer at the Web design firm Razorfish.

PHOTO CREDITS

Pp. 6, 19, 52 © AP/World Wide Photo; p. 11 © Petsmart.com; p. 24 © Michael S. Yamashita/Corbis; p. 32 © Catherine Karnow/Corbis; p. 42 © Monster.com.

SERIES DESIGN AND LAYOUT

Les Kanturek